Meditations to Soothe the Vagus Nerve

Get out of Fight or Flight and into a State of Rest, Digest and Heal

Wendy Hayden

SWH Media, LLC

Contents

1. Meditation and Your Vagus Nerve — 1

2. How to Implement a Meditation Practice into Your Daily Routine — 7

3. Meditation to Stimulate the Vagus Nerve — 11

4. Meditation to Calm Your Nervous System — 17

5. Meditation to Get Out of Fight or Flight — 21

6. Meditation to Improve Digestion — 25

7. Meditation to Release Anxiety — 29

8. Meditation to Release Anger — 33

9. Meditation to Release Fear — 37

10. Meditation to Release Resentment — 41

11. Meditation for Deep Sleep — 45

12. Meditation for Belonging — 49

13. Meditation to Reduce Inflammation — 53

14. Meditation for Healing — 57

15. Meditation for Autoimmune Disease   61

16. Meditation for PTSD   65

17. Meditation for IBS   69

18. Meditation for Constipation Relief   71

19. Meditation to Help Your Child Get Out of Fight or   75
     Flight

20. Meditation to Feel Safe   79

21. Meditation for Belonging   83

22. Meditation for Pain Relief   87

23. Make Meditation a Long Term Part of Healing Your   91
     Vagus Nerve

Chapter 1

Meditation and Your Vagus Nerve

The vagus nerve is the longest cranial nerve in the body and runs from the brain stem to the heart to the digestive system. It is the gut-brain connection. The vagus nerve is a key component of your emotional regulation, digestion, and heart rate. Known as the "wandering nerve" because it wanders throughout the body, the vagus nerve regulates the heart rate, digestion, and other bodily functions.

Unfortunately, because of a variety of factors, the vagus nerve can become damaged or weakened, leading to a variety of health issues. When it's not functioning properly, it can lead to issues like fatigue, digestive issues, depression, and more.

A part of the autonomic nervous system is the vagus nerve. The autonomic nervous system comprises the sympathetic and the parasympathetic nervous system. The sympathetic nervous system triggers the fight-or-flight response and puts your body into an alert, tense state when it perceives danger. The parasympathetic nervous system brings about a calming, restful state and is often referred to as the "rest and digest" state. Meditation can help to improve the body's ability to self-regulate, which is important for maintaining good health. Self-regulation is necessary for controlling blood pressure, heart rate, and other vital functions. Meditation can help to improve the body's ability to self-regulate, allowing the body to return to a state of balance more quickly.

Stress, fear, and other overwhelming emotions can trigger fight, flight, causing the body to go into a state of survival. When in this state, your body is in a heightened state of alertness, fear, and anxiety, limiting your ability to think clearly and act normally. This state of alertness can be beneficial in certain situations, but can also lead to long-term stress and physical illness if experienced too often.

When the vagus nerve is stimulated, it shifts you from a sympathetic state to a parasympathetic state and can help to reduce the body's response to stress, fear, and other overwhelming emotions. Stimulating the vagus nerve has been found to be beneficial in treating depression, anxiety, and other mental health issues, as well as gastrointestinal problems and heart issues.

There are many ways to stimulate the vagus nerve. Cold exposure, triggering the gag reflex, deep breathing exercises, humming, and meditation are some ways to stimulate the vagus nerve.

Meditation is an effective tool for calming the body and mind, resulting in a reduction of physical and mental stress. Meditation activates the parasympathetic nervous system, which helps to counter the autonomic nervous system's fight, flight, or freeze response.

Meditation is a practice that helps to quiet the mind and create a sense of stillness, allowing us to gain insight into our thoughts, feelings, and emotions. When we meditate, we can learn to observe our thoughts without getting caught up in them. This helps to reduce the intensity of our anxiety and develop a greater sense of mental and emotional balance. Meditation is essentially a practice of mindfulness, or the ability to be aware of your thoughts, feelings, and bodily sensations without judgment.

Meditation can help to reduce levels of cortisol, the primary stress hormone, in the body. This can help to bring our bodies back into a more balanced state and restore the vagal tone. When our vagal tone is balanced, we are better able to regulate our emotions and our physiological responses to stress.

Meditation also helps to reduce levels of inflammation in the body, which can help to reduce physical pain and discomfort. Additionally, meditation can help us to better cope with stressful situations and develop a more mindful approach to our lives. This can further help to reduce the stress and anxiety associated with the fight-or-flight response.

Meditation can be done in a variety of ways, such as with guided imagery, deep breathing, or progressive muscle relaxation. Guided imagery is a form of deep relaxation that can help to reduce stress and anxiety, while deep breathing helps to slow the heart rate and reduce blood pressure. Progressive muscle relaxation can help to relax the muscles in the body and reduce tension. All of these types of meditation can help to bring the body back into a more relaxed and balanced state and can help to stimulate the vagus nerve. , but the primary goal is to focus on your breath and become aware of your body and the present moment. Whether you prefer to sit in silence and focus on your breath or use guided meditation like those included in the book to help you relax, the goal is to create a sense of calmness and peace in your body and mind. When you are able to relax and reach a state of stillness, your body can better regulate its systems, including the vagus nerve.

We will explore some of the different types of meditations in the scripts included in this book. I encourage you to experiment with different types of meditation and try different scripts until you find one that works best for you.

Regardless of the type of meditation you choose, it's important to make it a part of your long-term healing plan. Regular meditation practice can help to reduce stress, improve mental clarity, and help you to stay calm and relaxed in the face of danger.

In the next chapter, we'll talk about ways to incorporate meditation into your healing regimen and make it a part of your daily practice.

Chapter 2

How to Implement a Meditation Practice into Your Daily Routine

Meditation is a powerful tool for improving your mental, emotional, and physical well-being. But it's challenging to keep up with a regular meditation practice when life gets busy. When your life is too busy to take time to meditate, that is when you need meditation the most.

Here are some ideas to help you get started on your own personal meditation practice.

1. Set a time: Set aside a specific time of day to meditate, and then stick to it. The best time to meditate is typically in the morning

before you start your day or in the evening when you're winding down.

2. Find a peaceful spot: Choose a space that is quiet and comfortable. This could be a corner of your bedroom, a cozy spot in your home, or even a park bench. Make sure to use comfortable clothing as well, since feeling too hot or cold can distract from your meditation practice.

3. Don't overthink it: Meditation doesn't have to be complicated. All you need is your breath and a comfortable seat. If you're feeling overwhelmed, just focus on your breath for a few minutes and clear your mind.

4. Create a routine: Create a meditation routine that works for you and stick to it. Try meditating for five to ten minutes every day and gradually increase the duration as you get more comfortable with the practice.

5. Be mindful: Be nonjudgmental about your practice and the thoughts that come up in your mind. Notice the thoughts, but don't get attached to them. Just let them pass by and go back to focusing on your breath.

6. Get support: If you're having trouble setting up a regular practice, get help from friends or family. Having someone to meditate with can often make it easier to stick with it.

7. Focus on Your Breath: During your meditation, focus your attention on your breath. Notice your inhales and exhales. Don't worry if your mind wanders, just bring your attention back to your breath.

8. Start Small: Don't expect to meditate for hours on end. Start off with brief sessions of five minutes and gradually increase your time as you become more comfortable. Meditating for a longer time isn't necessarily more effective.

9. Give Yourself a Break: Meditation won't always come easily. If you find yourself struggling, give yourself a break and come back to it another day.

Once you have established a regular meditation practice, you'll start to see the benefits it can have on your mental, emotional, and physical health. Give yourself time to adjust to your practice and remember to be patient and compassionate with yourself. Don't be discouraged if it takes some time to get used to the practice. It will become an easy and invaluable part of your daily routine, eventually.

If you're feeling like you're in fight, flight, or freeze mode, the first step is to take a few moments to relax and focus on your breath. Taking the time to focus on your breathing can help to bring your body back into a more relaxed and balanced state, which can help to stimulate the vagus nerve. Once you've taken a few moments to relax, you can then choose to practice some type of meditation.

The following meditation scripts will help you soothe your vagus nerve and get you out of flight, flight, freeze and into a state of rest, digest, heal.

Try the different scripts until you find one that resonates with you. You can use these meditation scripts anytime you are feeling overwhelmed or anxious.

Chapter 3

Meditation to Stimulate the Vagus Nerve

When you meditate, you're essentially stimulating the vagus nerve. When you meditate, your body relaxes and you're able to tap into the power of the vagus nerve, allowing it to regulate your heart rate, breathing, digestion, and other important functions. In addition to calming the body, meditation can also help to stimulate the vagus nerve in other ways. For example, it can help to increase activity in the prefrontal cortex, the region of the brain responsible for complex decision making and problem solving. This can help to improve mental clarity and focus, allowing people to make better decisions and solve problems more effectively.

The benefits of stimulating the vagus nerve through meditation are numerous.

Firstly, it can reduce stress and anxiety, as well as improve your mood. By stimulating the vagus nerve, you're helping to bring balance to your nervous system, allowing your body to relax and regulate its functions more effectively.

Furthermore, stimulating the vagus nerve through meditation can also improve heart rate variability. This is important as it helps to reduce the risk of developing cardiovascular disease. It can also help to reduce inflammation and improve digestion, both of which are important for overall health.

Finally, stimulating the vagus nerve through meditation can also help to improve concentration and focus. When you meditate, your brain is able to relax, allowing you to focus on the task at hand more easily. This can help to boost productivity and enable you to get more done in less time.

Start by finding a comfortable position, whether that's sitting in a chair or lying down.

Take a few moments to become aware of your breath and let it become deep and slow. Close your eyes and take a few deep breaths.

Now bring your attention to the area at the base of your neck, right between your collarbones. This is the area where the vagus nerve starts its journey through the body.

Take a few moments to imagine the energy of the vagus nerve flowing through this area. As you imagine the energy flowing, take a deep breath and allow your body to relax.

Now imagine a soft white light radiating from the base of your neck and traveling down the length of the vagus nerve.

As the light continues to travel, imagine it connecting to each of the organs and systems connected to the vagus nerve, bringing balance and calm to the body. Continue to focus on the soft white light traveling down the length of the vagus nerve and connecting to all the organs and systems. As you do, take a few moments to become aware of any sensations or changes in the body.

Inhale deeply through your nose, and exhale slowly through your mouth. Focus your attention on your breath and let go of any thoughts or worries that may be on your mind.

Feel your body relax as you exhale, and let your shoulders and neck muscles soften.

Now, focus on your breath.

As you inhale, concentrate on drawing the breath deep into your body, as if you're filling your chest and belly with air.

As you exhale, imagine that your breath is flowing outward and releasing any tension or stress.

Now, close your eyes and focus on the space between your eyebrows. Feel the area between your eyebrows relax and soften.

Take a few more deep breaths and imagine a soft light radiating from the area between your eyebrows. Allow this light to flow down your face and neck and then relax your chest and abdomen. Continue to breathe deeply and focus on the area between your eyebrows.

Bring your awareness to your throat as you focus on your breath. As you inhale, imagine the air entering your throat and circulating throughout your neck. As you exhale, feel the air exiting your throat and releasing any tension or tightness.

After a few breaths, bring your attention to your body. Notice any sensations in your body and any areas of tension. After a few moments of awareness, begin to relax any areas of tension by consciously encouraging your body to let go.

Visualize a wave of relaxation flowing through your body and feel your body progressively relax.

Now, imagine a string connecting your throat to the base of your spine. Visualize the string emitting a gentle vibration that travels down the string and into your body. Feel the vibration calming your body and mind.

Now, with each breath, silently recite the following mantra: "My vagus nerve is functioning optimally. I am relaxed, peaceful, and content."

Repeat your mantra on each inhalation and exhalation.

Continue to repeat this mantra for the next few minutes. As you repeat the mantra, focus on your breath and the sensation of your throat and neck muscles releasing any tension.

Notice how you feel, emotionally and physically.

Stay in this state of relaxation for as long as you like, allowing your body and mind to sink deeper into relaxation with each passing moment.

When you're ready, slowly open your eyes and take a few more deep breaths. Notice how you feel and how your body has responded to the relaxation.

Chapter 4

Meditation to Calm Your Nervous System

Meditation is a practice that can help you to focus your attention and achieve a state of inner peace and relaxation. When you meditate, you're essentially allowing your body and mind to come together in harmony. As you meditate, you're calming your nervous system and activating the parasympathetic nervous system, which is responsible for relaxation.

Our nervous system is incredibly complex and can be affected by so many things, including trauma and chronic stress. It's important to take time to relax and give your mind and body a break.

This meditation script can help you calm your nervous system and bring peace and relaxation to your body, mind, and spirit.

To begin, take a few moments to notice your physical sensations. Feel the pressure of your body on the chair or the floor, the temperature in the surrounding room, and the flow of your breath.

Now bring your attention to your breath. Feel the sensation of inhaling and exhaling as your breath naturally moves in and out.

Now take a few moments to focus on your body, from head to toe. Allow yourself to notice any areas of tension. Acknowledge any tension and then allow yourself to gently let it go.

Once you feel relaxed, focus on your breath.

Notice the rhythm of your breathing and the sensation of air entering and leaving your body. Feel the stillness that comes with a relaxed breath.

Now, take some time to envision a place that brings you peace and calm. It can be real or imagined. It doesn't matter - just choose a place that makes you feel relaxed and at ease. Once you've chosen your place, imagine yourself there.

Feel the sensation of relaxation that comes with being in this place. Spend some time here and really take in the sensations of relaxation and peace.

Now draw your awareness to your heart center and feel the sensation of your heart beating. Allow yourself to be soothed by the rhythm of your heart.

Now, shift your attention to your nervous system. Imagine that your nervous system is a river, with waves of energy rolling through your body. Feel the rhythm of the waves and take a few moments to connect with the energy of your nervous system.

Now, slowly release any tension in your body. Visualize the waves of energy slowly calming and the tension melting away. As the wave of relaxation passes, let go of all mental chatter and just focus on your breath.

Feel your body melting into the ground beneath you. Imagine a feeling of peacefulness radiating through your body.

Allow yourself to sink deeper into the stillness of this moment. Feel your body becoming more and more relaxed as you surrender to the stillness.

As you continue to relax, feel the sensation of peace and contentment that comes with the calmness of your nervous system. Feel your body and mind coming into harmony.

When you are ready, slowly move your awareness back to your breath. Feel the sensation of inhaling and exhaling, and the peace that comes with each breath.

Take a few moments to sit in this peaceful state.

When you are ready, slowly open your eyes and take a few moments to savor the peace that you have created. Take this feeling of peace and calm with you as you go through your day.

Chapter 5

Meditation to Get Out of Fight or Flight

The fight-or-flight response is an instinctive response to perceived danger or threat, and it's difficult to shut off once something has triggered it. Fortunately, meditation can be an effective way to help you get out of this state of heightened alertness and back into a relaxed, balanced state of mind.

This meditation script is designed to help you get out of fight-or-flight and back into a more peaceful and relaxed state of being.

Before you begin, be sure to find a comfortable, quiet place where you can relax without interruption. Once you are settled, let's begin.

Start by taking a few moments to bring your awareness to your body. Notice how it feels to sit in this space and the sensations of your body as it rests in this moment.

Now, close your eyes and take slow, deep breaths. Notice any feelings or sensations of fear or anxiety. Observe these feelings without judgment, simply recognizing them for what they are.

Take a few moments to focus on your breath, allowing the breath to relax and soothe the body. As you continue to focus on your breath, imagine that the fear or anxiety is slowly melting away.

As you do so, imagine a warm, white light entering through your nose, filling your body and radiating out to the tips of your toes and the top of your head. This light is a reminder of peace and calm.

As you continue to breathe, bring your focus to your heart. Notice how it feels to be here, in this moment, and allow yourself to let go of any worries or stress. Letting go of any fear that is present.

Now, imagine that your heart is a beautiful, glowing sphere of light. Notice how this light radiates out, filling the room and your body with a sense of peace and calm.

Now, imagine a rope connecting your feet to the ground.

This rope is a symbol of your vagus nerve. Feel the strength, stability, and security this connection brings.

Next, imagine the rope connecting your hands with the energy of the rope flowing through your arms and into your heart, bringing a feeling of love and compassion.

Finally, visualize the rope connecting the top of your head with the energy of the rope flowing through your body and out into the universe. Feel the energy of this connection fill your entire being.

You can easily shift out of fight-or-flight mode and into a more relaxed state of being.

Continue to stay here, in this peaceful state, for as long as you need. As you do, imagine that you are tapping into a deep well of inner strength, courage, and resilience.

When you are ready, slowly open your eyes and bring your awareness back to the present moment. Notice how you feel, and if necessary, take a few moments to ground yourself back into the present.

Chapter 6

Meditation to Improve Digestion

In addition to calming the mind and body, meditation can also help to improve the communication between the brain and the gut. This is because the vagus nerve plays an important role in the gut-brain axis, which is the bidirectional communication between the gut and the brain. Through meditation, we can help to strengthen this connection and improve communication between the two.

For improving digestion, there are many meditation techniques that can be used. One of these techniques is called guided meditation. This type of meditation involves following a script that helps you focus and relax. Here is a meditation script specifically designed to help improve digestion.

Let's take a few moments to settle in and get comfortable in this moment. If you're sitting, make sure your spine is tall and your shoulders are relaxed. You can put your hands on your lap, palms face up or down. If you're lying down, let your body sink into the ground and find a comfortable position.

Breathing in, breathe in the peace and relaxation of the present moment.

Breathing out, release any tension or worries.

Allow your body to become relaxed, your muscles to soften.

Taking a deep breath in, and a long breath out, feel the surrounding space, and the stillness of the moment.

Allow your breath to become your ally in this meditation, and focus on your breath as it moves in and out, in and out. Feel the air entering and leaving your body, and notice the sensations of the breath in your chest, belly, and around your lips.

As you continue to breathe, focus on the feeling of relaxation, and scan through your body, noticing any areas of tension. Take a few moments to soften any areas of tension and let go of any thoughts or worries.

Now, focus your attention on your belly. Imagine a warm, relaxing, golden light filling your belly. As you continue to focus on this light, allow yourself to become aware of the sensations of your digestion. Notice the contraction and expansion of your stomach and intestines, the slow and steady movement of food through your digestive system.

Take your time to observe your belly and its functions without judgment or criticism. Now, with each breath, imagine that the golden light is expanding and healing your digestive system. Feel it filling your body with warmth and energy.

Visualize this light slowly healing and restoring any parts of your digestive system that may be feeling out of balance. Let the light fill your entire body with a sense of peace and relaxation.

As you continue to focus on your breath and the light in your body, repeat the following phrase to yourself:

"My digestive system is healthy and strong. I am relaxed and at peace."

With each repetition, allow yourself to feel more and more relaxed. Let the light in your body continue to restore balance and harmony.

"My digestive system is healthy and strong. I am relaxed and at peace."

"My digestive system is healthy and strong. I am relaxed and at peace."

Visualize the digestive process from the moment you take a bite of food through the process of digestion to the elimination of waste from the body.

Imagine your food being broken down and absorbed into the body, and your body being able to get the nutrients it needs from your food.

As you visualize this process, focus on your breath. With each inhalation, imagine the air being filled with relaxation and healing energy. With each exhalation, allow this energy to flow through your body, especially through your digestive system.

Picture the relaxation energy circulating through your digestive system, relieving any tension and discomfort. Visualize your digestive system functioning at its best, with all the parts working together harmoniously.

Continue to focus on your breath and visualize your digestive system functioning optimally.

Allow yourself to be here, in this present moment, and feel the peace and relaxation that comes with this. Take a few more moments to continue to let go, as you allow your body to rest and digest.

When you're ready, slowly open your eyes, taking a few moments to adjust to the space around you. As you move through your day, let the peace and relaxation that you experienced in this meditation stay with you.

Chapter 7

Meditation to Release Anxiety

We all experience moments of anxiety and stress throughout our lives. That's why having a meditation script to release anxiety can be so helpful. A meditation script can provide a calm, soothing way to quiet the mind and take a break from the stress of the moment. This meditation script for anxiety helps you find peace and relaxation in the present moment.

The goal is to practice being in the present moment by focusing on your breath and being mindful of your thoughts and feelings.

To begin, find a comfortable position in a chair or seated on the floor.

Close your eyes and take a few deep breaths.

As you inhale and exhale, notice the sensation of the breath in your body. Feel the sensation of your chest and abdomen rising and falling as you breathe in and out.

Now, bring your attention to your thoughts. Notice any anxious or fearful thoughts that arise without judging them or trying to change them.

Now, imagine that your worries, anxieties, and fears are like clouds in the sky. Notice the clouds, but don't get attached to them. Acknowledge them and let them pass.

Imagine your worries floating away.

Imagine your anxieties floating away.

Imagine your fears floating away.

With each breath, imagine these emotions floating away

Now, bring your attention to the area of your body where you are feeling the most tension and anxiety.

Notice the tension and simply observe it without judgment. Breathe into the area, allowing the breath to release the tension. As you continue to breathe, imagine that the tension is melting away with each exhale.

When you are ready, notice the sensation of the breath as it moves in and out of your body.

As you inhale, imagine that the breath is bringing in a sense of calm and peace. As you exhale, imagine that the breath is releasing any anxious or fearful thoughts. Continue to focus on your breath and notice any changes in your body. Notice any lightness or heaviness in your body, any tightness or relaxation in your muscles.

We are now going to use a positive mantra to reaffirm your commitment to relaxation and peace. You can repeat these mantras silently to yourself or aloud as part of your meditation.

"I am relaxed, peaceful, and at ease."

"I am relaxed, peaceful, and at ease."

"I am relaxed, peaceful, and at ease."

"I am strong and capable of managing my anxiety."

"I am strong and capable of managing my anxiety."

"I am strong and capable of managing my anxiety."

"I am safe and I can let go of my worries."

"I am safe and I can let go of my worries."

"I am safe and I can let go of my worries."

Continue to focus on your breath until you find yourself in a state of deep relaxation.

When you are ready, slowly open your eyes.

Take a few moments to bring your attention back to the present moment.

Allow yourself to slowly move your body and gradually come back to the here and now.

Take a few more deep breaths and recognize that you have the power to find peace and relaxation in the present moment.

Chapter 8

Meditation to Release Anger

Anger is a powerful force that can help us protect ourselves and respond to danger, but it can also lead to overreaction and unnecessary negative emotions. By using a meditation script to release anger, you can take a step back and observe your thoughts and feelings, allowing you to gain insight into the source of your anger.

This script is designed to reduce the physical effects of anger and activate the parasympathetic nervous system, which helps promote healing and relaxation. We will focus on releasing anger and connecting with the vagus nerve, also known as the fight, flight, or freeze response. This response handles our body's reaction to stress, fear, and danger. When we get stuck in the fight portion of fight, flight, freeze, it can cause many mental and physical health problems.

To begin, find a comfortable position, either sitting or lying down.

Close your eyes and take slow, deep breaths. As you inhale, imagine a wave of soothing energy moving through your body, starting at the top of your head and moving down through your neck, shoulders, and chest. As you exhale, imagine the stress and tension leaving your body.

Visualize the nerve stretching from the base of your skull all the way down to your diaphragm. Visualize the nerve becoming more active and engaging.

As you focus on this nerve, imagine the energy of anger running through it.

Now, take a few moments to connect with the source of your anger.

Acknowledge the emotion and allow yourself to fully experience it.

Now, bring your attention to the sensations of anger, frustration, or irritation that are present in your body. Notice where they are located and allow yourself to simply observe them.

Acknowledge and accept any anger you feel without judgment.

Now, focus on the source of your anger.

Remember the situation or person who made you angry. Notice the thoughts, emotions, and physical sensations that arise in your body.

Allow yourself to feel these emotions without judgment or resistance.

Take a few moments to imagine how you would like to feel instead. As you do, imagine that your vagus nerve is releasing the energy of anger, allowing it to dissipate and move out of your body.

On each out-breath, soften your body around the sensation of anger. As you do this, imagine that the sensation is slowly releasing from your body. Continue to breathe deeply and with each out-breath, allow the sensation to slowly melt away.

Now, focus your attention on the space that is left behind. Allow yourself to fill this space with compassion, understanding, and acceptance. Continue to breathe deeply and focus your attention on the space that is left behind. Now, give yourself permission to release any remaining anger, frustration, or irritation. With each out-breath, allow yourself to let go of any negative emotions that remain.

Focus your attention on any physical sensations, such as a tingling in your limbs or a warmth throughout your body. With each breath, imagine the relaxation spreading throughout your body and the anger dissipating.

Imagine a ball of light in your hands. Visualize the light growing brighter and brighter until it is so bright that it is almost blinding.

Imagine the bright white light filling your body. This is the light of peace and calm that will help to dissipate the anger and wash away all the negative energy and emotions.

Visualize the light slowly spreading throughout your body, starting from your head and traveling down to your toes. As it passes through your body, the anger dissipates and you feel calmer and more at peace. Continue to visualize the light and allow yourself to feel the peace and quiet that it brings.

Continue to breathe deeply and allow the relaxation to fill your body.

Focus on the feeling of peace and calm that is now present in your body. Visualize yourself in a calm and peaceful place.

Take a few moments to relax and soak up the feeling of peace and contentment. When you are ready, open your eyes and give yourself a few moments to come back to the present.

Chapter 9

Meditation to Release Fear

We all experience fear in our lives, and it can often be overwhelming and difficult to manage. Fear can come in many forms, like fear of failure, fear of the future, fear of the unknown, or fear of rejection. By learning how to tap into mindfulness and meditation, we can become better equipped to manage and even lessen our fear.

This meditation script is designed to help you to release your fear and find more peace and calm in your life.

Begin by finding a comfortable position, either seated or lying down.

Close your eyes and focus your attention on your breath. As you inhale, feel your chest, belly and rib cage expand. As you exhale, feel the tension releasing from your body.

Allow your body to relax and let go of any tension or stress.

Now, focus on the fear that is present within you. Notice how it feels in your body. Identify the parts of your body that feel uncomfortable, tense, or tight.

As you notice the fear, imagine it gradually flowing out of your body and dissipating into the atmosphere.

Now, bring your attention to the area of your body where you felt fear the most. It could be your stomach or chest, or any other area of your body. Focus on this area and notice how your body feels at this moment. Is it tight? Is it relaxed?

Allow yourself to experience whatever sensations arise without judgment.

Now, imagine that fear is a deep pool of energy located in this area of your body. Take a few moments to visualize this energy and feel its intensity. Now, release this fear from your body.

Allow yourself to surrender to the process. You may feel a physical or emotional release, or you may simply feel a sensation of peace.

As you release the fear, notice any beliefs that may be associated with it. Allow yourself to let go of any stories, judgments, or patterns that arise.

Now, focus on what you want to feel instead of fear. Visualize a feeling of peace and relaxation, filling your body with calm and soothing energy.

Imagine yourself in a safe and protected space, feeling safe and secure. This could be a place in nature, a beach or a mountain, or a room of your own. Imagine yourself in this peaceful place and feel the warmth and safety that it brings.

Now, bring your awareness to the area in your body where the fear is located. Notice how it feels and the sensations that come with it. Let the fear be there, but don't judge it or push it away. Notice how it affects your body.

Now, bring your attention to your breath.

As you inhale, imagine a warm, golden light coming into your body, melting away the fear and calming your mind. As you exhale, imagine releasing the fear and all the accompanying thoughts.

Continue to breathe and focus on the light, allowing it to fill your body and bring peace and calm.

Now, take a few moments to sit with this feeling of peace and calm, noticing how it affects your body and mind.

When you're ready, slowly open your eyes.

Take a few moments to look around and to consider how you're feeling. Take this feeling of peace and calm with you throughout your day and use it to help you move through moments of fear.

Chapter 10

Meditation to Release Resentment

Resentment can be a powerful emotion. It can lead to feelings of anger and helplessness, and can prevent us from being our best selves. Do you feel like you're carrying around the weight of resentment due to something that has happened in the past? Maybe you can't seem to let go of the hurt and anger you feel towards someone else and it's keeping you from feeling truly free. Resentment can also be a hard emotion to let go of, but with practice and intention, we can move away from that negative place.

To begin, take a few moments to sit in stillness and observe your breath. Feel each inhale and exhale, and allow yourself to notice your body.

Now, bring your attention to the area of your body where you feel resentment. Notice how it feels in your body, and what emotions and thoughts come up when you think about it. Notice the sensations you feel in your body -- tension, tightness, heat, or cold. Take a few moments to focus on these sensations as you explore them. Don't be afraid of what you feel--just observe it and acknowledge it.

Now, imagine that the resentment you are feeling is a heavy weight that is pressing down on your body. Notice how the weight feels and the sensations it creates.

Picture a balloon. The balloon is filled with all the resentment you're carrying, and it's slowly growing bigger and bigger as you fill it with more and more resentment.

Now imagine a large white light surrounding the balloon.

With each breath, the light grows brighter and brighter, until it completely envelopes the balloon. Visualize the light slowly melting away the resentment. With each breath, the light loosens the grip of resentment, and it drifts away from you.

Finally, imagine the balloon rising into the sky and disappearing.

Now, allow yourself to let go of the resentment and anger. Imagine that the weight is slowly lifting away from your body, leaving you feeling lighter and freer.

As the weight lifts away from you, notice how the feelings of resentment and anger change. Notice how the intensity of the feelings begins to lessen and eventually fades away.

Now, imagine you are holding a soft, white light in your hands. Feel the warmth of the light, and imagine it radiating out and surrounding your body. Allow the light to fill your body with a feeling of warmth and compassion.

As the feelings fade away, take a few moments to just sit with the feelings of peace and freedom that come up in their place. Allow yourself to enjoy the feeling of liberation and freedom.

Take a few moments to observe the sensation of your body without the resentment. Feel the warmth, peace, and openness that comes with it.

Notice how the weight of resentment and anger has lifted away and how you feel a sense of inner freedom and peace. Let this feeling of peace and freedom be your reminder that you are strong enough to let go of the past and move forward with a lighter heart.

Finally, when you're ready, slowly open your eyes. Take a few moments to appreciate the peaceful feeling that comes with releasing resentment.

Chapter 11

Meditation for Deep Sleep

Meditation is a great way to relax your body and mind and get a good night's sleep. This meditation script for deep, restful sleep will help you to relax and drift off into a restful and restorative sleep.

Before we begin, lie down on your bed and close your eyes.

Focus on your breathing and allow yourself to relax into the moment. Feel your body become heavy and sink into the bed beneath you.

Feel the air entering your nose and filling your lungs. When you exhale, feel your chest and abdomen relax, and your body sink further into the ground. Take one more deep breath and let it out as a sigh.

Allow yourself to relax even deeper into the bed.

As you meditate, pay attention to any thoughts that come into your mind. Acknowledge these feelings without judgment and then return your focus to the sensation of your breath. Feel the air entering your nose and filling your lungs. As you exhale, feel your chest and abdomen relax, and your body sink further into the ground.

As you continue to breathe, feel your muscles begin to soften and your mind and body drift away into a peaceful state.

Now, begin to focus on the sound of your breath. Hear each inhale and each exhale. Listen to the rhythm of your breath and allow yourself to become deeply relaxed.

Begin to imagine a warm, comforting light surrounding you. Feel a sense of safety and relaxation as the light envelops your body.

Notice the rise and fall of your abdomen as you breathe in and out. Observe the rhythm of your breath without trying to change it. Allow your breath to become slow and steady.

Begin to count each inhalation and exhalation backward from 10.

As you count, allow your body to relax even more.

9

8

7

6

5

4

3

2

1

When you reach zero, begin again. As you count, allow your body to relax even more.

10

9

8

7

6

5

4

3

2

1

0

Continue this practice until you feel your body and mind relax completely.

Now, take a few more deep breaths and imagine that you're falling asleep.

Feel yourself drifting off into a deep and restful sleep. When you feel you've reached a deep state of relaxation, you will allow yourself to drift off to sleep knowing that you'll wake up feeling refreshed and rejuvenated.

Place your hand on your chest and bring your attention to your heartbeat. Feel the rhythm of your heart beating. Let this slow, steady rhythm carry you into a deep and restful sleep.

Chapter 12

Meditation for Belonging

I n this session, we will explore how to cultivate an inner sense of connection and belonging within yourself, so that it can radiate outward and be shared with the wider world.

First, find a comfortable position and close your eyes. Take a few moments to settle into your body and get comfortable. Allow your body to relax and sink into the ground, feeling the support beneath you.

Take a few moments to simply observe the breath and notice what thoughts come up.

Take a few deep breaths in and out. Feel your breath travel through your body, allowing yourself to feel grounded, safe, and secure.

Now, imagine a place that you feel a deep sense of belonging. This can be a physical location, such as a childhood home, or it can be a mental space, like a happy memory.

Wherever it is, take some time to explore this place in detail. Notice the sights, sounds, smells, any emotions that come up, and any sensations in your body as a result of these.

Notice what you are feeling in your body. Allow yourself to feel whatever emotions come up. Embrace them and bring them into your heart. Remind yourself that you are worthy of feeling a sense of belonging and connection.

Now, bring your awareness to the energy of your heart. Feel the warmth of your heart and open to the possibility of feeling a sense of belonging.

Imagine yourself surrounded by a circle of beautiful, supportive, and loving people. Feel the warmth of their love and acceptance for you. Notice how their presence brings you a sense of security and belonging.

Allow yourself to relax into the feeling of being in this circle. Notice the warmth and compassion radiating from these people. Feel the sense of connection and belonging that they offer. Breathe deeply and receive their love. Feel the peace and security that comes with knowing you have a place to belong.

Now, imagine the energy of the group moving outward and surrounding you in a field of unconditional love. Feel the warmth of this energy wrap around you and fill you with a feeling of belonging.

Allow yourself to savor this feeling. Allow yourself to receive the love and acceptance of the group. Feel the feeling of support, security, and belonging become stronger inside of you. Feel the energy of belonging that you have cultivated and allow it to expand outward. Notice how this feeling radiates outward and connects you to something larger than yourself.

Sense how it can help you feel part of the human experience.

Stay here with this feeling for a few moments, allowing yourself to be embraced by the energy of love and acceptance. Give yourself permission to take this feeling of belonging with you wherever you go. Take a few more deep breaths in and out. Invite this feeling of belonging to stay with you throughout your day.

Now, slowly return your attention to the breath and gently open your eyes. Take a few moments to sit with this feeling of connection and belonging and let it permeate your being.

When you're ready, you can move on with your day, feeling more connected and at ease in your body and soul.

Chapter 13

Meditation to Reduce Inflammation

Meditation is a powerful tool for reducing inflammation, a state that can lead to various health problems. Inflammation is a natural and beneficial response which helps protect us from injury and infection, yet when it is out of balance, it can cause chronic pain, exhaustion, and other ailments. Conditions associated with inflammation include pain, rigidity, and other symptoms linked to chronic diseases, such as arthritis, lupus, and fibromyalgia. Stress, poor diet, and other lifestyle choices can also be causes of inflammation.

Fortunately, meditation can reduce inflammation and its associated symptoms. Through regular meditation, you give your body the opportunity to heal and restore itself.

Here is a simple meditation script:

Find a comfortable spot to sit or recline. Close your eyes and take several deep breaths. Bring your attention to your breathing.

Notice the sensations of your breath as it enters and exits your body.

Now bring your attention to your body and scan it for areas of tension or discomfort. Notice any areas of inflammation that you can feel. Notice how the inflammation feels, and how it affects your body.

Take a few moments to visualize the inflammation as a bright, vibrant color. Picture it growing more intense and bright with each breath.

Now, imagine the color shifting and changing, becoming softer and more muted. Imagine the soothing golden light entering your body in these areas. This light is the healing power of the Universe and it is here to help reduce the inflammation.

As this light enters your body, direct it to the areas of inflammation and imagine it healing and soothing the inflammation. Feel the area becoming soft and relaxed as the light and healing energy gently melts away the inflammation.

Continue to focus on the light entering your body and healing the inflammation.

Feel the pain and discomfort fading away as the light works its magic. Continue to breathe deeply and focus on the soothing, healing light until you feel the inflammation has been reduced.

Bring your attention to the center of your chest. Visualize the warm, calming light filling your chest. Allow the light to spread throughout your body, bathing your cells in its warmth.

Notice the warmth and allow it to penetrate any areas of inflammation.

Take a few deep breaths and notice the way each breath feels in your body. As you continue to breathe, notice how your body relaxes. Feel the inflammation melting away, as if it were melting away under the warmth of the sun. Continue to focus on your breath and the relaxing feeling in your body as the inflammation fades away.

Take a few moments to focus on the sensations of warmth and relaxation.

Picture the inflammation reducing and your body healing itself.

When you're ready, open your eyes and take a few more deep breaths. Notice how your body feels and how much of the inflammation has been reduced. Take a moment to thank yourself for taking the time to reduce the inflammation in your body. You deserve to feel good and to enjoy your life without the pain and discomfort of inflammation.

Chapter 14

Meditation for Healing

With this meditation script, you will be taken on an inner journey to a place of healing and peace. Take your time and be gentle with yourself as you go through this meditation.

Begin by finding a comfortable, quiet space where you can be alone and uninterrupted.

Close your eyes and take a few deep breaths, allowing your body and mind to relax.

Focus your attention on your breath. Feel the air moving in and out of your lungs. Notice the sensation of the air passing through your nostrils and the sensation of your chest rising and falling with each breath.

As you continue to breathe, become aware of the sensations in your body. Notice any areas of discomfort or tension. Take a few moments to consciously relax any areas of tension. As you do this, imagine a healing energy emanating from your breath and entering these areas of tension.

Visualize a beautiful, peaceful place. It can be a beach, a forest, a garden, or any other place that brings you a sense of peace and tranquility. As you continue to breathe deeply, imagine yourself in this place. Notice the colors, sounds, smells, and feelings that this place brings to you.

Allow yourself to sink into the peace and relaxation of this place. Feel the soothing energies it brings to you. Imagine that these energies are healing and nourishing you, restoring balance and harmony in your body and mind.

Spend some time in this place, allowing the energies to flow through you, restoring balance and harmony.

Now, bring your focus to any emotional pain or distress you may be experiencing.

Take a few moments to sit with this feeling and acknowledge it. Then, imagine this feeling being washed away with each breath, replaced with a feeling of peace and well-being.

As you continue to breathe, repeat these affirmations with me, either silently or out loud.

"I am healing with every breath I take,"

"I am strong and capable of healing,"

"I am surrounded by love and healing energy."

Now, take a few moments to visualise a bright healing light.

Imagine the light is entering your body through the crown of your head and flowing down through the rest of your body. Allow the light to fill your body with a feeling of warmth and healing. Feel it seeping into every cell, bringing a sense of wholeness and balance.

As the light continues to flow, imagine that it is washing away any negative thoughts, emotions, or memories that have been holding you back. Visualise them being carried away by the light, dissolving and releasing their hold on you.

Allow yourself to feel the sensation of being healed. Feel the nourishment of the light as it flows through your body, bringing peace and wellbeing.

Stay in this state of awareness for as long as you need, and then slowly bring your attention back to the present moment. Take a few deep breaths and gently open your eyes, feeling refreshed and energized.

Take a few moments to feel the effects of the meditation, and to journal any insights or feelings that arise.

Chapter 15

Meditation for Autoimmune Disease

Autoimmune disorders occur when the body's own immune system attacks the body's own cells and tissues, leading to inflammation and pain. One of the more recent medical applications of meditation has been in reversing auto-immune disorders, such as lupus, rheumatoid arthritis, Crohn's disease, and multiple sclerosis.

By meditating regularly, people can reduce stress and improve the body's immune system, which can in turn help to reverse the symptoms of auto-immune diseases.

Take a few moments to become comfortable and relaxed in your meditation space.

Inhale deeply and slowly, allowing your body to expand and relax on the exhale. Bring your attention to your breath, noticing the sensations of the breath entering and leaving the body.

Take time to become aware of your body and the sensations taking place within.

Allow the breath to move through the body, gently releasing any tension or blockages.

As you continue to breathe deeply, focus your attention on your body, noticing any areas of tension. As you pay attention to any areas of tension, imagine a warm, soothing light slowly filling these areas, helping them to relax and release.

Now, focus your attention on your abdominal area, the area around your belly button. Imagine a warm, peaceful energy radiating from this area. Feel the warmth, and allow it to spread outwards to the other areas of your body. As the warmth reaches each area, imagine it filling those areas with healing energy, helping to reduce inflammation.

Continue to focus your attention on the warmth of your abdominal area and allow it to spread further out across your body. Feel the warmth as it spreads, helping to reduce inflammation, and aiding in your body's natural healing process.

Now, visualize a beautiful white light surrounding your body, a light that is filled with love, healing energy, and protection. As this white light envelops your body, feel it healing and protecting you from any further inflammation or damage.

The healing light is permeating your cells and tissues with warmth and healing. Feel the healing light entering every cell in your body, restoring life and balance to the auto-immune system. Imagine the healing light cleansing any toxins, and slowly healing the immune system.

Imagine this white light healing and repairing any damaged cells or tissues in your body. Feel the energy of the white light entering your body and bringing peace and relaxation.

Visualize this white light pushing out any negative thoughts or feelings that you may be having.

Allow this healing light to remain with you as you continue to meditate.

Finally, spend a few moments reflecting on how this meditation experience has made you feel. Notice any changes that may have occurred within you, such as feeling more relaxed or having more energy. Allow yourself to remain in this peaceful state of mind for as long as you need to. When you're ready, slowly bring your awareness back to the room and to your breath. Thank yourself for taking the time to meditate and for the healing taking place.

Chapter 16

Meditation for PTSD

PTSD can often feel like an overwhelming and unmanageable experience. Symptoms of PTSD may include difficulty sleeping, intrusive memories, hyper-arousal, and avoidance. Meditation can be a powerful tool for managing the symptoms of PTSD.

Begin by finding a comfortable position. You can be sitting or lying down.

Close your eyes and take a few deep breaths. Feel the air entering your lungs and exiting your body.

Now, focus on your body. Scan your body from head to toe. Notice any areas of tension or tightness. Take a few deep breaths and let the tension go.

Now, bring your awareness to your heart. Imagine a warm, white light radiating from your heart. Allow this warm light to fill your body with a sense of safety and calm.

Next, bring your awareness to your breath. Notice the rhythm of your breath and focus on the sensation of air entering and exiting your body. Inhale peace and exhale any tension or stress. Allow yourself to relax into the rhythm of your breath.

Focus on each breath and allow yourself to relax into the moment.

Now bring your attention to the surrounding sounds. Listen to any noises that come and go and just observe them without judgment.

As you continue to focus on your breath, slowly notice any physical sensations you may be feeling. Notice any areas of tightness or tension and take a few moments to relax and soften those areas.

Now, take your awareness inward and focus on your emotions. Notice any feelings that arise and take a few moments to observe them without judgment. Notice the sensations they bring and allow them to be without trying to push them away.

Now, imagine yourself in a peaceful place of your choosing. This can be a beach, a mountain, a forest, or anyplace else that brings you comfort and peace. Take some time to explore this place, noticing the colors, smells, and sounds that it offers. Feel the warmth and safety of this place and allow yourself to relax into the peace and tranquility it offers.

Stay in this place for as long as you'd like and then, when you're ready, slowly come back to the present moment. Notice the sights, sounds, and smells around you. Let go of any thoughts or worries that come up.

Notice the peace and stillness that surrounds you. When you are ready, slowly move your body and open your eyes. Notice any changes you may have experienced during the meditation. Take this peace and calm with you into your day.

Meditation for IBS

Meditation can be an effective way to reduce stress, which can be a major contributor to IBS symptoms. Meditation can help with IBS symptoms, as it has been shown to reduce symptoms such as abdominal pain, bloating, and constipation.

Here's a simple yet effective meditation script for IBS symptom relief:

Find a comfortable position and close your eyes.

Allow your thoughts and worries to drift away.

Notice your body. Notice any tension or discomfort.

Focus on your breath and follow its rhythm.

Imagine that you're breathing in healing energy and breathing out any discomfort or pain. Take slow, deep breaths. Imagine that the breath is a healing balm, soothing your body and relieving any tension.

Continue to focus on your breath and the healing energy moving through your body. On each exhale, relax a little more deeply. Healing energy enters your body, soothes your digestive system, and calms down any IBS-related symptoms.

Take slow, deep breaths and imagine that each inhalation brings in healing energy and each exhalation releases any discomfort or pain. Focus on taking slow, deep breaths while picturing a healing balm soothing your body and relieving any tension.

Visualize a warm, healing light pouring into your body and melting away any discomfort or pain. Imagine the energy entering your body and calming IBS-related symptoms. Allow the light to gently bring a sense of peace and relaxation, making your body feel lighter and more at ease.

By taking the time to focus on your breath and visualize a calming place, you can help to relax your body and mind and reduce IBS symptoms, allowing you to find relief. Regularly practicing this meditation can also help to reduce stress and keep your IBS symptoms at bay.

Chapter 18

Meditation for Constipation Relief

Meditation is an effective and natural way to relieve consti-pation and promote regular bowel movements. It can help you relax, reduce stress, and increase your awareness of your body and its needs. By using a guided meditation script, you can target the physical and mental causes of constipation while also calming your mind.

This script can help you relax and clear your mind, allowing your body to relax and focus on its natural processes.

Begin by finding a comfortable position. You may sit or lie down in whatever way is most comfortable for you.

Close your eyes and take deep, slow breaths. As you inhale, focus on the air going into your lungs. As you exhale, focus on the air going out. Notice the sensation of the air as it enters your body and follows its path of air back out of your body. Allow yourself to relax into the rhythm of your breathing.

Feel your abdomen as it rises and falls with each breath. Notice any tightness, tension, or discomfort. As you continue to focus on the sensation in your abdomen, imagine a wave of relaxation flowing through your body. With each breath, allow the wave to build, slowly creating a wave of relaxation and comfort throughout your body. With each breath, feel your body becoming more relaxed and your digestion becoming more efficient.

While breathing deeply, visualize a white light entering your body. Feel the warmth and comfort of this light as it travels through your body. Notice how it brings peace and relaxation with it.

When you feel completely relaxed, focus on your digestive system.

Envision your entire digestive system, from your stomach all the way down to your intestines. Visualize the muscles working together to push the food down the digestive tract. Imagine that your digestive system is working to its fullest potential, allowing for the maximum absorption of nutrients. Visualize the waste in your body being flushed away.

Now, bring your awareness to any blockages or tightness in your abdomen. As you breathe, imagine the tightness melting away, allowing the relaxation wave to move through your abdomen more freely. Continue to imagine the wave of relaxation moving through your abdomen until it reaches the area of your colon.

Notice any tightness or discomfort in the area of your colon.

Again, imagine the wave of relaxation moving through the area, allowing the tightness to release. Continue to focus on the wave of relaxation as it travels through your abdomen and colon. Allow the wave of relaxation to continue to move through your body, relaxing any other areas of tension.

Now, focus on the part of your digestive system that is blocked. Picture the food being stuck and unable to move. Visualize it slowly melting away, and the blockage being released.

Feel the relief and relaxation as the blockage is cleared.

Continue to take deep, slow breaths while visualizing the process of your digestive system working normally. Feel the tension and stress melting away and the energy flowing freely through your body.

Finally, with each breath, imagine the wave of relaxation spreading to your entire body, allowing it to relax deeply.

Take a few moments to sit in stillness, noticing the sensations in your body and the feelings of relaxation and comfort that linger.

When you are ready, slowly open your eyes and return to the present moment.

By using this simple meditation script for constipation relief, you can help your body naturally relax and move the food through your digestive system. By taking the time to practice this meditation script for constipation relief, you can promote healthy digestion and reduce your symptoms. With regular meditation practice, you will notice lasting improvements in your digestive health.

Chapter 19

Meditation to Help Your Child Get Out of Fight or Flight

Meditation can help children become more aware of their emotions and surroundings, and can also help reduce stress and anxiety. Meditation is a wonderful way to help children relax and find peace of mind. It can help them develop a healthy sense of self-awareness and self-regulation, as well as cultivate an attitude of acceptance and understanding.

As parents, it's important to equip our children with the tools they need to manage their stress and emotions. Meditation is an incredibly powerful tool for helping kids become calmer and more centered.

When our children are in a state of fight, flight, or freeze, they are in a state of heightened alertness and stress; their bodies and minds are on high alert, and they are trying to protect themselves from potential threats. In these moments, our children are in survival mode; their goal is not to feel better, but rather to protect themselves from harm.

The goal of meditation for our children is to help them transition out of this state of fight, flight, or freeze and into a more relaxed state of rest, digest, and heal. This allows them to access a more balanced and regulated state of mind and body, enabling them to better manage their emotions and respond to stressful situations in a more healthy way.

When helping our children to move out of fight, flight, or freeze, it is important to create a safe and calming environment. This can be done by providing a peaceful space in which they can relax and by speaking to them in a supportive and nurturing way. Once the environment is set, it is then important to guide our children through a meditation script that is tailored to their needs.

This guided meditation script is designed to help your child move out of fight, flight, or freeze and into a state of rest, digest, and heal. It's important to explain the process to your child, and provide them with instructions on how to do the meditation.

Start by having your child sit in a comfortable position, either cross-legged on the floor, lying on their bed, or sitting in a comfortable chair.

Take a few moments to settle in, allowing your body to relax and your breath to become even.

Next, take a few moments to focus on your breath. Notice your breath as it moves in and out of your body. Notice the sensation of the breath, where in your body you feel your breath the most. Observe your breath as it moves in and out of your body. Now, begin to expand your awareness of your entire body. Notice any areas of tension or tightness and gently bring your attention to them.

Visualize a gentle flow of energy, like a warm liquid, melting away the tension.

As you continue to focus on your body, bring attention to your heart. Feel a sense of love and compassion for yourself. Picture a golden bubble of light surrounding your body.

Notice any thoughts or feelings that come up. These thoughts and feelings do not have to be acted upon, but simply acknowledged.

Now, imagine a safe and peaceful place. This could be a beach, a meadow, or a special spot in your house. Visualize this place in vivid detail, including what you see, feel, hear, and smell.

Once you can clearly picture your peaceful place in your mind's eye, imagine a path that you can walk on, winding its way through the beautiful scenery. This path can have any shape or direction that you choose.

As you follow the path, notice the different sensations in your body. Focus on the senses in your body until you reach the end of your path.

When you arrive at the end, take a few moments to just be in this peaceful place, breathing in the calming energy.

When you are ready, open your eyes and return to the present moment.

If needed, repeat this meditation script multiple times throughout the day.

Meditation can help our children to gain more control over their emotions, to better manage stress, and to develop healthy coping strategies for times of difficulty. By practicing this meditation regularly, your child will be better equipped to manage their emotions and stay in a state of rest, digest, and heal.

Chapter 20

Meditation to Feel Safe

Meditation is a wonderful way to relax and create a sense of safety. No matter what you're facing, meditation can bring you a sense of calm and protection from the outside world.

Find a comfortable seated position and close our eyes. Take a few moments to settle in and let go of any tension in your body.

The following script will help you do just that.

Take a few deep breaths, closing your eyes and focusing on your breath. As you inhale, notice your breath coming in, and as you exhale, notice your breath going out. With each breath, allow yourself

to feel more relaxed and safe. Allow yourself to become more and more relaxed.

As you continue to focus on your breath, bring your awareness to your body as a whole. Notice any sensations that arise as you observe your body. Now, notice if any of these sensations are bringing up any feelings of fear or anxiety. Allow yourself to be with these feelings without judgment. Feel the tension slipping away and the calmness that comes with it. Allow your body and mind to become still, your thoughts become quiet, and your worries drift away.

Visualize yourself in a safe and secure place--somewhere that brings you peace. It could be a place in nature, a special spot in your home, or any other place that makes you feel secure.

Imagine yourself in that space and notice how it looks, how it feels, and what it smells like. Allow yourself to explore this safe space. Notice any details that stand out to you. Feel the warmth of the sun, feel the coolness of the breeze, and take in the views around you.

This is your safe space.

Let go of all expectations and allow yourself to be in the moment.

Allow yourself to simply be here in this safe place, free of stress and worry. Immerse yourself in the feelings of safety and security, and notice how they affect your body and mind.

Visualize yourself feeling more relaxed and at ease. Continue to take deep breaths in and out and focus on the feeling of safety. Feel the peace that comes with this feeling, and how it brings comfort to your body and mind.

Take a few moments to really appreciate the feeling of safety and security. Feel the comfort of being in a safe place and how it allows your body and mind to relax.

Feel the safety and security that comes with knowing this place. Allow yourself to be in this space, feeling protected and secure.

Take as much time as you need to be in this safe space.

Now, imagine that a bubble of protection surrounds you.

This bubble is made up of whatever makes you feel safe and secure. It can be a physical sensation, such as a warm hug or a specific color. It can also be a spiritual presence, such as an angel or a divine being.

Once you have identified what makes you feel safe, take a few moments to imagine being surrounded by this bubble of protection. Notice how this bubble of protection creates a sense of security.

Allow yourself to relax and feel safe within this bubble. As you continue to meditate, repeat this mantra to yourself: "I am safe and secure." Each time you repeat this mantra, feel the sensation of safety and security grow within you.

When you are ready, bring your awareness back to your breath. Notice the sensation of your breath coming in and out. Take a few more deep breaths, and when you are ready, slowly open your eyes. Remember that this safe place is always there for you, and you can always return to it whenever you need to.

Chapter 21

Meditation for Belonging

This meditation script is designed to help you connect with yourself and the people and places around you in a meaning-ful and comforting way. It can help you create a sense of belonging and connection that can help you through difficult times. In this meditation, you'll explore the powerful healing effects of being connected to others and to your environment, and how it can help you live with a greater sense of purpose and wholeness.

Begin by finding a comfortable position. You can sit, stand, or lie down.

Close your eyes, and take a few deep breaths to ground yourself. Feel the rise and fall of your chest, the stillness in between each breath, and

the expansiveness of your lungs. As you settle into this moment, notice your breath and make a conscious effort to relax your body and mind.

We'll start with a grounding exercise.

Take a moment to focus on your body. Notice the sensation of your feet on the ground, your body against the chair, or your hands in your lap. Feel the physical connection between you and the surrounding environment.

Imagine that you have roots that extend deep into the earth below. Feel the energy of the earth coming up into your body, nourishing and calming your body with each breath you take.

Now, bring your attention to your breath. Notice the sensation of your breath as it moves in and out of your body. Feel the air touching your skin as you breathe in and out.

Now, bring your attention to your heart. Imagine a bright, warm light radiating from your heart. This light is a source of connection and belonging. You can use this light to connect with yourself and the people and places around you. As you imagine this light radiating out of your heart, feel a sense of connection and belonging.

Know that you are not alone.

Now, bring your awareness to the energy of the wider world. Feel the energy that is shared between all living beings, and know that you are a part of this interconnected network of life.

You are part of this world.

You belong here.

Now, bring your awareness to the energy of the earth that supports us. Feel the stillness and quiet of the land, and know that you are a part of this great and ancient cycle of life.

Now, bring your attention back to your breath. Notice the sensation of your breath as it moves in and out of your body. Feel the air touching your skin as you breathe in and out.

When you are ready, take a few moments to open your eyes and come back to the present. Take a few deep breaths to ground yourself.

Now, take a moment to reflect on the sense of connection and belonging that you experienced during this meditation. Remember that it is always there, and that you can come back to it at any time.

Take a few moments to sit in stillness before slowly transitioning back into your day. Carry with you the feeling of belonging and connectedness that you've cultivated during this meditation.

Remember, you are not alone.

Chapter 22

Meditation for Pain Relief

If you're suffering from chronic pain, meditation can help you find relief. Studies have shown that meditation can reduce pain, decrease anxiety, and improve overall wellbeing. It can help to reduce the intensity of pain, reduce its duration, and even prevent it from returning.

With meditation for pain relief, the goal is to help you become more aware of the present moment, to focus on the here and now and accept the moment as it is.

This meditation script for pain relief will help you relax and reduce your experience of pain. Take a few moments to get into a comfortable position. Some people find it helpful to sit in a chair with their feet flat on the floor. If that's not comfortable for you, you can lie down on your back.

Close your eyes and focus your attention on your breath. Notice the sensation of the air as it enters and leaves your body. Notice the rise and fall of your chest and belly with each breath.

Now, direct your attention to the area of your body where you're experiencing the pain.

Notice the sensation without trying to change it. Simply notice and accept it as it is.

Now, imagine that the pain is like a wave. Allow it to come and go, without pushing against it. As you do this, visualize warm, healing energy traveling to the painful area.

Imagine that it is soothing and calming the pain.

Continue to observe the pain without judgment. Allow yourself to accept it without resistance.

As you continue to relax, let go of any thoughts and emotions that are associated with the pain.

Release any tension in your body and allow yourself to relax deeper.

Imagine a soft, warm light radiating from any remaining areas of pain. Picture the light as a balm, gently soothing the area and allowing it to relax. As the light continues to expand, allow it to spread throughout the body.

Now, imagine the sensation of the pain dissipating, slowly and gradually.

Visualize the pain slowly melting away and being replaced by a sensation of relaxation.

Continue to focus on your breath and imagine the pain slowly disappearing. Notice how the area of pain is becoming lighter and more relaxed with each breath.

Now, imagine a wave of relaxation washing over your entire body, calming every cell and muscle. Allow the wave to wash away any tension and stress.

Imagine that the pain is slowly fading away, replaced with a sense of well-being and inner peace. Allow yourself to relax more deeply and to enjoy the feeling of peace and relaxation.

Now, let's move on to visualizing a comfortable and safe place. Imagine a place where you feel secure and relaxed. It can be a favorite spot in nature or a place you have only visited in your dreams. As you relax into this space, imagine the pain and tension fading away.

Allow yourself to let go and experience a deep sense of peace and relaxation. As you do, if you notice any negative thoughts or feelings, simply acknowledge them and let them pass.

Take some time to stay in this state of relaxation and peace.

Finally, take a few moments to bring your awareness back to the present moment. Notice the sounds in the room, the sensations in your body, and the stillness inside you.

When you're ready, slowly open your eyes and come back to the room. Take with you the sense of relaxation and peace that you've cultivated.

Whenever you need pain relief, you can use this meditation script. You can practice it anywhere and anytime. You can practice it for a few minutes or for a longer period. By using this meditation script for pain relief, you can find relief from your chronic pain and bring more peace and relaxation into your life.

Chapter 23

Make Meditation a Long Term Part of Healing Your Vagus Nerve

Making meditation a part of your long-term healing of your vagus nerve is one of the best ways to keep your body and mind in balance. By taking the time to sit in stillness and practice meditation, you can give your body the rest and relaxation it needs to function optimally.

When you practice meditation regularly, you will see the benefits it has on your vagus nerve. You may experience improved digestion, better emotional regulation, and a reduction in stress and anxiety. As your practice grows, you find that the benefits of meditation become more profound.

Meditation is an ancient practice that has been used for centuries to bring peace and healing to people's lives. It is a powerful way to bring balance and harmony to the mind and body, reducing stress and restoring balance.

Besides the guided meditations included in this book, there are other types of meditation that can help regulate your vagus nerve, such as body scan, mantra, or visualization meditation, that you can practice on your own. You can write your own scripts, either using the ones in this book as a base or start from scratch.

There is no right or wrong way to practice meditation. Find works best for you.

Taking the time to cultivate a regular meditation practice can be a powerful act of self-care and a great way to stay balanced and healthy. Self-care is essential for the health of your vagus nerve, so make time for activities that make you feel relaxed and nurtured.

It may take some time to get used to meditating, but it's important to be patient and consistent in order to see the best results. Be kind and gentle with yourself when meditating. Don't judge yourself if your mind wanders, or if it takes time to get used to the practice. Allow yourself to be present in the moment and trust that the practice is helping you to heal your vagus nerve.

By taking the time to make meditation a part of your long-term healing of your vagus nerve, you can feel the positive effects of the practice. Meditation can have an almost immediate effect on your mental and physical health, but it may take some time for you to feel the full benefits. Don't get discouraged if you don't see results right away. Remember, meditation isn't a one-size-fits-all solution. What works for one person may not work for another. Take your time to find a practice that resonates with you and take whatever steps you need to make it part of your long-term healing plan. With consistent practice, you can feel more relaxed, more connected to your body, and more in control of your overall health and wellbeing.

When you practice meditation regularly, you can see the benefits it has on your vagus nerve. You may experience improved digestion, better emotional regulation, and even a reduction in stress and anxiety. As your practice grows, you find that the benefits of meditation become more profound.

Making meditation a part of your long-term healing of your vagus nerve is one of the best ways to keep your body and mind in balance. By taking the time to sit in stillness and practice meditation, you can give your body the rest and relaxation it needs to function optimally. Meditation is one of the most powerful tools we have for healing, and when it comes to healing the vagus nerve, it can be an invaluable part of a long-term healing journey.

There are other therapies besides meditation that can help to support your vagus nerve health, such as cold therapy, tapping, and humming. I discuss these alternative therapies in more depth in my book, The Vagus Nerve: Gut Brain Connection.

www.ingramcontent.com/pod-product-compliance
Lightning Source LLC
Chambersburg PA
CBHW070816170726
48000CB00018B/931